Let's Look at Presidents

by Luana K. Mitten and

Rourke
Educational Media

rourkeeducationalmedia.com

Rocks can be very small. Rocks can be very big.

Sand is made of tiny pieces of rock.

You can hold pebbles in your hand.
A pebble is a rock that is about the size
of a pea.

Stones are bigger than pebbles. You can find stones in a stream.

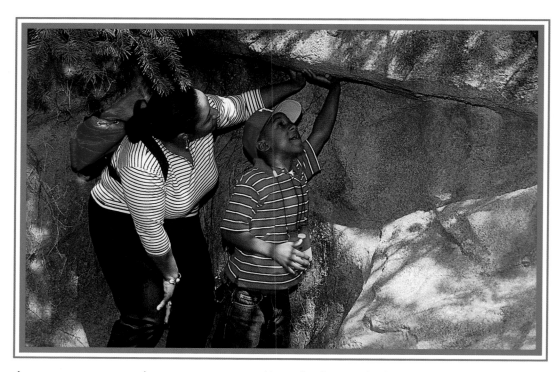

Larger rocks are called boulders.

If you climb big rocks and boulders,
be careful.

We can **chip** and **carve** small rocks.

The Lincoln Memorial, Washington, D.C.

We can chip and carve big rocks.

Wind and water wear away rocks. Caves are formed. Some are large enough to build homes inside.

Mesa Verde National Park, Colorado

We build chimneys with rocks. Rocks will not **melt** from the heat in the chimney.

Continental Army's winter huts at Valley Forge Military Park, PA.

Rocks are strong. We build walls
with rocks.

We can stack rocks. A **pyramid** is made of stacked rocks.

General George Washington Memorial at Mount Vernon

We can pave paths and yards with rocks.
Aren't rocks a useful part of our world?